Airplanes

by Lola M. Schaefer

Bridgestone Books

an imprint of Capstone Press
Mankato, Minnesota

Bridgestone Books are published by Capstone Press
818 North Willow Street, Mankato, Minnesota 56001
http://www.capstone-press.com

Library of Congress Cataloging-in-Publication Data
Schaefer, Lola M., 1950–
Airplanes/by Lola M. Schaefer.
    p. cm.—(Transportation library)
    Includes bibliographical references and index.
    Summary: An introduction to airplanes, discussing how they fly, the main
components to a plane, early models, and interesting facts.
    ISBN 0-7368-0358-0
    1. Airplanes—Juvenile literature. [1. Airplanes.] I. Title. II. Series.
TL547.S333   2000
629.133'34—dc21   99-13168
                                                                              CIP

Editorial Credits

Mari C. Schuh and Blanche R. Bolland, editors; Timothy Halldin, cover designer
   and illustrator; Heather Kindseth, illustrator; Kimberly Danger, photo researcher

Photo Credits

Archive Photos, 14
Continental Airlines, 8–9
Corbis, 12–13, 16–17
Frederick D. Atwood, 18
Photophile/Richard Cummins, 4; Tom Tracy, 6, 8 (inset)
Visuals Unlimited/Bruce Berg, cover; A&E Morris, 20

**Bridgestone Books thanks F. Robert van der Linden of the National Air and Space
Museum at the Smithsonian Institution for reviewing this book.**

Table of Contents

Airplanes

Airplanes are a fast way to travel. Powerful engines move airplanes through the air. Passengers take airplanes to travel long distances. Passengers get on and off airplanes at airports.

passenger
someone other than the driver who travels in a vehicle

Traveling by Airplane

Passengers buy tickets from an airline. At the airport, passengers check in at the airline desk. They board the airplane at an airport gate. Pilots fly the airplane. Flight attendants keep passengers safe and comfortable.

airline

a company that owns airplanes and flies passengers to many places

cockpit

wings

tail

engine

cockpit

Parts of an Airplane

Most airplanes have the same main parts. An airplane has a long body. An airplane has two wings and a tail. Engines power airplanes. An airplane has a cockpit. Pilots use controls in the cockpit to fly the plane.

jet airplane

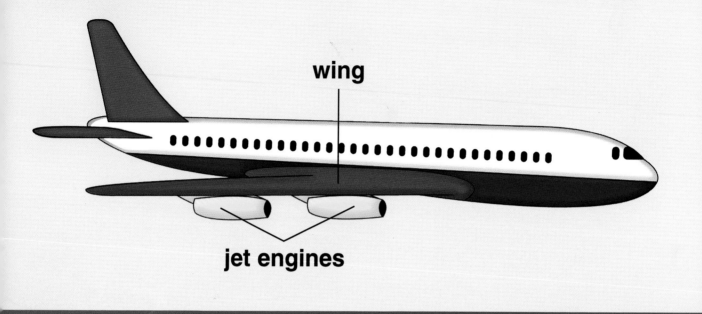

wing

jet engines

propeller airplane

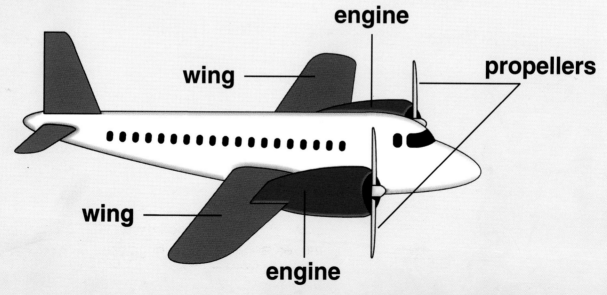

engine

propellers

wing

wing

engine

How an Airplane Flies

An airplane's engines and its shape help it to fly. Engines on some small airplanes turn propellers. Engines on large jet airplanes push hot gases away from the engines. The shape of the wings helps lift airplanes into the air.

propellers
a set of turning blades that moves an airplane through air

Before the Airplane

Transportation was slow before airplanes were invented. People traveled across land in horse-drawn buggies, on trains, or in cars. Ships were the only way to cross the oceans. Airplanes can travel fast over land and water. Trips that once took days on land now take only hours by airplane.

The Inventors of the Airplane

Orville and Wilbur Wright were bicycle makers. The Wright brothers made the first engine-powered airplane. In 1903, Orville flew the *Wright Flyer* at Kitty Hawk, North Carolina. The plane was in the air for only 12 seconds during its first flight.

Early Airplanes

Early airplanes were made of cloth, wood, and wire. They often had more than two wings. The first passenger airplanes were old World War I (1914–1918) planes with extra seats. Great Britain and Germany developed the jet engine during World War II (1939–1945).

Airplanes around the World

People around the world use airplanes. Most countries have airports. Many remote places have small airports. Small airplanes transport people to larger airports. Airplanes help people work and travel anywhere in the world.

remote
far away or hard to reach

The Concorde

Airplane Facts

- The Concorde is a supersonic airplane. It travels at about 1,450 miles (2,330 kilometers) per hour. This speed is more than twice the speed of sound. The Concorde can cross the Atlantic Ocean in less than three hours.

- Most jet airplanes travel at 600 miles (966 kilometers) per hour.

- In 1927, Charles Lindbergh became the first person to fly alone across the Atlantic Ocean. His flight from New York City to Paris, France, took 33.5 hours.

- A Boeing 747 passenger airplane has about 4.5 million parts.

- Pilots fly most airplanes above the clouds. Flights are usually smooth because airplanes fly above the weather.

Hands On: Make a Model Engine

Jet engines move airplanes forward with a force called thrust. You can learn how thrust works.

What You Need

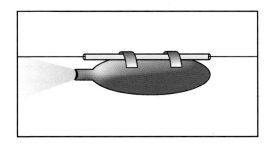

Piece of string 10 to 16 feet
  (3 to 5 meters) long
Drinking straw
Long, thin balloon
Tape
Helper

What You Do

1. Tie one end of the string to a doorknob or drawer handle.
2. Put the other end of the string through the straw.
3. Pull the string tight. Tie it to another doorknob or drawer handle at least 9 feet (2.7 meters) away.
4. Move the straw near one end of the string.
5. Blow up the balloon. Pinch the end of the balloon closed. Place the balloon underneath the straw.
6. Have a helper tape the balloon to the straw.
7. Step back and let go of the balloon.

Air coming out of the balloon pushes it forward along the string. The stream of air works like the thrust of a jet engine.

Words to Know

comfortable (KUHM-fur-tuh-buhl)—to be relaxed and free from worries

engine (EN-juhn)—a machine that makes the power needed to move something

flight attendant (FLITE uh-TEN-duhnt)—a person who keeps passengers safe and comfortable during an airplane trip

inventor (in-VENT-ur)—a person who thinks of and makes something new

jet engine (JET EN-juhn)—an engine that is powered by a stream of gases made by burning fuel and air inside the engine

pilot (PYE-luht)—a person who flies an airplane

transportation (transs-pur-TAY-shuhn)—a system of moving people and things from one place to another

Read More

Berger, Melvin and Gilda Berger. *How Do Airplanes Fly?* Discovery Readers. Philadelphia: Chelsea House Publishers, 1998.

Otfinoski, Steven. *Taking Off: Planes Then and Now.* Here We Go! Tarrytown, N.Y.: Benchmark Books, 1997.

Stille, Darlene. *Airplanes.* A True Book. New York: Children's Press, 1997.

Internet Sites

Aero Design Team Online: What Is Aeronautics
http://quest.arc.nasa.gov/aero/background/#howflies

Aeronautics—Parts of an Airplane
http://www.allstar.fiu.edu/aero/fltmidparts.htm

Milestones of Flight
http://www.nasm.edu/GALLERIES/GAL100/gal100.html

Index